Laurence Binyon

Lyric Poems

Laurence Binyon

Lyric Poems

ISBN/EAN: 9783744718806

Printed in Europe, USA, Canada, Australia, Japan

Cover: Foto ©Thomas Meinert / pixelio.de

More available books at **www.hansebooks.com**

Lyric Poems

By Laurence Binyon

Elkin Mathews & Jo: Lane
London: 1894

NOTE.

THE poems in this volume are arranged, as far as possible, according to the time of their composition, or conception ; the first dates from 1887, the last from 1893. A few have appeared before, in the *Academy*, the *Oxford Magazine*, the *Hobby Horse*, &c. Four, Nos. I., VI., IX., and XIV., were published in "Primavera" (Blackwell ; Oxford, 1890).

INDEX OF FIRST LINES.

IN CARISSIMAM MEMORIAM

A. S. P.

To whom but thee, my youth to dedicate,
My youth, which these few leaves have sought to save,
Should I now come, although I come too late,
Alas! and can but lay them on thy grave?

To whom but thee?   From thee, I know, they stole
Their happiest music, all their finer part:
O could they breathe but something of thy soul,
Something of thine incomparable heart!

What was there lovely, that thou didst not love?
What troubled spirit could ever grasp thy hand,
Nor know what answering springs within thee strove
To soothe his wound; to feel, to understand?

A

Too much hadst thou of pain, and fret, and care ;
Yet surely thou wast meant for joy : to whom
Life, that had given thee days so hard to bear,
Could still yield moments of so rare a bloom.

That longing in me, which can never sleep,
To live my own life, to be bravely free,
What is that longing, but the passion deep,
The sweet endeavour, to be true to thee ?

Still in my mind the solemn morning shines ;
Still with me, ah, too clearly pictured, dwell
The day, the hour, with all their mournful signs,
When we bade thee, O friend of friends, farewell.

Austerely fair, the vast cathedral, filled
With February sunshine, marbles old,
Pillar on pillar, arch on arch revealed :
The light, the stillness, on my grief took hold ;

Hushed within those gray walls, that could not change,
Where kneeling sorrow heavenly comfort hears;
Appeased by their eternal strength, that, strange
Itself to pain, permitted human tears.

There that worn heart, those arms in longing strained
Beyond, beyond, toward the unknown shore,
Entered repose, their long-loved peace attained.
Sweetly she sleeps.   O shall we wish her more?

I climbed the high tower, up steep stairs of stone.
Under the clear sun plains without a wave,
Various and busy, in the morning shone:
The world about me, but below, thy grave.

White flowers marked it. Now, my flowers' poor grace
I bring, to bloom or fade; I little care.
Ah, let them fade, and die in that dear place!
It is enough, if they have faded *there*.

I.

PSYCHE.

She is not fair, as some are fair,
Cold as the snow, as sunshine gay:
On her clear brow, come grief what may,
She suffers not too stern an air;
But, grave in silence, sweet in speech,
Loves neither mockery nor disdain;
Gentle to all, to all doth teach
The charm of deeming nothing vain.

She joined me: and we wandered on;
And I rejoiced, I cared not why,
Deeming it immortality
To walk with such a soul alone.
Primroses pale grew all around,
Violets, and moss, and ivy wild;
Yet, drinking sweetness from the ground,
I was but conscious that she smiled.

B

The wind blew all her shining hair
From her sweet brows; and she, the while,
Put back her lovely head, to smile
On my enchanted spirit there.
Jonquils and pansies round her head
Gleamed softly; but a heavenlier hue
Upon her perfect cheek was shed,
And in her eyes a purer blue.

There came an end to break the spell;
She murmured something in my ear;
The words fell vague, I did not hear,
And ere I knew, I said farewell;
And homeward went, with happy heart
And spirit dwelling in a gleam,
Rapt to a Paradise apart,
With all the world become a dream.

Yet now, too soon, the world's strong strife
Breaks on me pitiless again;
The pride of passion, hopes made vain,
The wounds, the weariness of life.

And losing that forgetful sphere,
For some less troubled world I sigh,
If not divine, more free, more clear,
Than this poor, soiled humanity.

But when, in trances of the night,
Wakeful, my lonely bed I keep,
And linger at the gate of Sleep,
Fearing, lest dreams deny me light;
Her image comes into the gloom,
With her pale features moulded fair,
Her breathing beauty, morning bloom,
My heart's delight, my tongue's despair.

With loving hand she touches mine,
Showers her soft tresses on my brow,
And heals my heart, I know not how,
Bathing me with her looks divine.
She beckons me; and I arise;
And, grief no more remembering,
Wander again with rapturous eyes
Through those enchanted lands of Spring.

Then, as I walk with her in peace,
I leave this troubled air below,
Where, hurrying sadly to and fro,
Men toil, and strain, and cannot cease:
Then, freed from tyrannous Fate's control,
Untouched by years or grief, I see
Transfigured in that child-like soul
The soiled soul of humanity.

II.

A CHILD in nature, as a child in years,
If on past hours she turn remembering eyes,
She but beholds sweet joys or gentle tears,
Flower hiding flower in her pure memories.

So flower-like, so lovely do they seem:
Too fair to be let die, they fade too fast;
Not like that hopeless beauty, which in dream
Is ever present, but to say 'tis past.

Then should I come with sorrow at my breast,
Profitless sorrow, vainly wished away,
Will she give comfort to my heart's unrest,
She, whose bright years are as a morn of May?

Though I should sigh, I could not choose but cheer,
Knowing Joy is not far, when she is near.

III.

AN APRIL DAY.

BREEZES strongly rushing, when the North-West stirs,
Prophesying Summer to the shaken firs;
Blowing brows of forest, where soft airs are free,
Crowned with heavenly glimpses of the shining sea;
Buds and breaking blossoms, that sunny April yields;
Ferns and fairy grasses, the children of the fields;
In the fragrant hedges' hollow brambled gloom
Pure primroses paling into perfect bloom;
Round the elm's rough stature, climbing dark and high,
Ivy-fringes trembling against a golden sky;
Woods and windy ridges darkening in the glow;
The rosy sunset bathing all the vale below;
Violet banks forsaken in the fading light;
Starry sadness filling the quiet eyes of night;
Dew on all things drooping for the summer rains;
Dewy daisies folding in the lonely lanes.

IV.

A DIALOGUE.

The Man.

O TYRANNOUS ANGEL, dreadful God,
Who taught thee thus to wield thy rod?
So jealous of a happy heart,
Thou smot'st our happy souls apart,
And chosest too the weaker prey,
Refusedst the worthier foeman!

The Angel.

Nay:
I am my Master's minister.
Why ravest? · Peace abides with her.
Thou, who wast held in human thrall,
For thee I made the fetters fall;
I loosed thy bonds, I set thee free:
Now, thou regret'st thy liberty!

And why for what is cold repine?
She is no longer aught divine!
Can those chill lips, now purpled, speak?
Is any bloom upon that cheek?
Nay, if thou wilt, an idle kiss
I grant thee; that is all.

The Man.

Not this,
Not this I ask; but, Angel, give,
Give back the life that let me live!
Or take away this useless breath:
Grant me her consecrated death!
Where she has past, the way is pure,
If anything of good endure.

The Angel.

Fool, dost thou think to raise thy hand
Against the law no passion planned,
Or seek to shake the stars' repose
With crying of thy puny woes?

Turn to thy petty ways, and there,
There learn the wisdom of despair.

The Man.

O pitiless word! Yet slay me too:
Be kind, O Death! for my soul grew,
Watered and fed by gracious dew,
Till in one hour Love met with thee.
Now, the wide world is misery!

The Angel.

Love, who is Love? I know him not.
Strange things are ye, that learn your lot
So soon, and yet must needs bemoan,
When stricken with the fate foreknown.
Art thou more worthy, Man, to keep
Thine age from the appointed sleep,
Thy strength from the sure-coming hour,
Than the perfection of a flower!
They ask not for their lovely bloom
Exemption from the final doom;
And man, so full of fault and flaw,
Shall he evade the unchanging law?

Let him be wise; and, as the flowers,
With joy fulfil his destined hours,
Live with unanxious ample breath,
And when at last he comes to death,
Compose his heart and calm his eye,
And, proud to have lived, scorn not to die!

V.

NIOBE.

"Zeus, and ye Gods, that rule in heaven above,
  Is there nought holy, or to your hard hearts dear?
  Have ye forgotten utterly to love,
  Or to be kind, in that untroubled sphere?
  If aught ye cherish, still by that I pray,
  Destroy the life that ye have cursed this day!

"No, ye are cold!   The pains of tenderness
  Must tease not your enjoyed tranquillity.
  How should ye care to succour or to bless,
  Who have not sorrowed and who cannot die?
  Wise Gods, learn one thing from ephemeral breath;
  They only love, who know the face of Death.

"When did ye ever come as men to earth
  Save to bring plagues, war, misery, to us?
  O vanity!   We have smiled, yet know that birth
  Looks but to death through passions piteous.

While calm ye live, and when these human seas
Wail in your ears, feel deepest your own ease.

"Yet envied ye my keener happiness,
That ye must quench it in such triple gloom?
For, by a mercy more than merciless,
Slaying my children in their guiltless bloom,
Me ye slew not, but suffered, as in scorn,
Accurst to linger in a land forlorn.

"Where are they now, those dead, that once were mine?
I saw them in their beauty, thought them fair,
And in my pride dreamed they were half divine.
An idle boast I made, to my despair:
For in that hour they died, and I receive
A fate thrice bitterer, since I live to grieve."

So, on the mountains, hapless Niobe,
With feverish longing and rebellion vain,
Bewailed herself, swift plunged in misery,
Bewailed her children, by dread deities slain;
Those jealous deities, whose bright shafts ne'er miss,
Phœbus, and his stern sister, Artemis.

Nine days those bodies of unhappy death
Lay in their beauty, by Ismenus flood;
For on sad Thebes Zeus breathed an heavy breath,
And men became as marble, where they stood.
Nine suns their unregarded splendour shed;
And still unburied lay those lovely dead.

But on the tenth day the high Gods took pity,
And in the fall of evening from their seats
In heaven, came down toward the silent city,
The still, forsaken ways, the unechoing streets:
And through the twilight heavenly faces shone.
But no man marvelled; all yet slumbered on.

The king sat, brooding in his shadowy halls,
His counsellors ranged round him. With fixed eyes,
Set brows, and steadfast gaze on the dim walls,
He sat amid a kingdom's mockeries;
And seemed revolving many a thought of gloom,
Though his mind slept, and knew not its own doom.

The Gods beheld unheeding, and went through,
And came to the stream's side, where slept the dead.

And while stars gathered in the lonely blue,
They buried them, with haste and nothing said;
Feeling, perchance, some shade of human years,
And what in heaven is nearest unto tears.

So, their toil ended, the Gods passed again,
Through the deep night, to pale Olympus hill.
But in their passing breathed upon all men,
And loosed the heavy trance that held them chill.
Slowly night waned; the quiet dawn arose:
And Thebes awoke to daylight and her woes.

But Niobe, the mother desolate,
Enduring not to see her home forlorn,
To wander through the vacant halls, that late
Echoed with voice and laughter all the morn,
A homeless queen, went sorrowing o'er the hills,
Alone with the great burden of her ills.

There as she wept, a sleep was sealed on her;
Yet not such sleep as can in peace forget.
The strivings vain of hands that cannot stir,
And swelling passion, poisoned with regret,

And piercing memory, in their dark control
Possess with torment her imprisoned soul.

She, clouded in her marble, seeming cold,
Majestically dumb, augustly calm,
Yet feeling, through all bonds that round her fold,
A nameless fever that can find no balm,
A grief that kindles all her heart to fire,
The crying of a tyrannous desire,

Remains for ever mute, for ever still.
Thebes marvels, gazing at the stony thing,
And deems it lifeless as the barren hill,
To which the winds and rains no bloom can bring:
Yet under that calm front burns deeper woe
Than ever Thebes, with all her hearts, can know.

No hope she sees in any springtime now,
But it is buried in with the autumn leaves.
Yet, when day burns upon her weary brow,
Deadened to her deep pain, she scarcely grieves;
And, burdened with the glory of that great light,
Almost forgets it brought her children night.

But when the pale moon makes her splendour bare,
Terrible in the beauty of cold beams,
The radiance falls on the mute image there,
And Niobe awakens from her dreams.
Those subtle arrows search her soul, with pain
Tenfold more cruel from her children's bane.

Remembering their dead faces, she would sigh :
But the pure marble brooks no sound of grief.
She only lives to sorrow silently,
And, in despair, still hope some last relief.
The Gods are stern ; and they to those long years
Ordained an immortality of tears.

VI.

TESTAMENTUM AMORIS.

I CANNOT raise my eyelids up from sleep,
But I am visited with thoughts of you;
Slumber has no refreshment half so deep
As the sweet morn, that wakes my heart anew.

I cannot put away life's trivial care,
But you straightway steal on me with delight;
My purest moments are your mirror fair;
My deepest thought finds you the truth most bright.

You are the lovely regent of my mind,
The constant sky to my unresting sea;
Yet, since 'tis you that rule me, I but find
A finer freedom in such tyranny.

Were the world's anxious kingdoms governed so,
Lost were their wrongs, and vanished half their woe!

C

VII.

As in the dusty lane to fern or flower,
Whose freshness in hot noon is dried and dead,
Sweet comes the dark with a full-falling shower,
And again breathes the new-washed, happy head:

So when the thronged world round my spirit hums,
And soils my purer sense, and dims my eyes,
So grateful to my heart the evening comes,
Unburdening its still rain of memories.

Then in the deep and solitary night
I feel the freshness of your absent grace,
Sweetening the air, and know again the light
Of your loved presence, musing on your face,

Until I see its image, clear and whole,
Shining above me, and sleep takes my soul.

VIII.

THE evening takes me from your side;
The darkness creeps into my breast.
Swift clouds across the dim heavens glide,
And fill me with their vague unrest.

I wander sad, and know not why:
The lighted streets perplex my brain.
I wish for wings, that I might fly
From sound and glare, to you again.

IX.

YOUTH.

When life begins anew,
And Youth, from gathering flowers,
From vague delights, rapt musings, twilight hours,
Turns restless, seeking some great deed to do,
To sum his fostered dreams; when that fresh birth
Unveils the real, the thronged and spacious Earth,
And he awakes to those more ample skies,
By other aims and by new powers possessed:
How deeply, then, his breast
Is filled with pangs of longing! how his eyes
Drink in the enchanted prospect!   Fair it lies
Before him, with its plains expanding vast,
Peopled with visions, and enriched with dreams;
Dim cities, ancient forests, winding streams,
Places resounding in the famous past,
A kingdom ready to his hand!
How like a bride Life seems to stand

In welcome, and with festal robes arrayed!
He feels her loveliness pervade
And pierce him with inexplicable sweetness;
And, in her smiles delighting, and the fires
Of his own pulses, passionate soul!
Measure his strength by his desires,
And the wide future by their fleetness,
As his thought leaps to the long-distant goal.

So eagerly across that unknown span
Of years he gazes: what, to him,
Are bounds and barriers, tales of Destiny,
Death, and the fabled impotence of man?
Already, in his marching dream,
Men at his sun-like coming seem
As with an inspiration stirred, and he
To kindle with new thoughts degenerate nations,
In sordid cares immersed so long;
Thrilled with ethereal exultations
And a victorious expectancy,
Even such as swelled the breasts of Bacchus' throng,
When that triumphal burst of joy was hurled
Upon the wondering world;

When from the storied, sacred East afar,
Down Indian gorges clothed in green,
With flower-reined tigers and with ivory car
He came, the youthful god;
Beautiful Bacchus, ivy-crowned, his hair
Blown on the wind, and flushed limbs bare,
And lips apart, and radiant eyes,
And ears that caught the coming melodies,
As wave on wave of revellers swept abroad;
Wreathed with vine-leaves, shouting, trampling onwards,
With tossed timbrel and gay tambourine.

Alas! the disenchanting years have rolled
On hearts and minds becoming cold:
Mirth is gone from us; and the world is old.

O bright new-comer, filled with thoughts of joy,
Joy to be thine amid these pleasant plains,
Know'st thou not, child, what surely coming pains
Await thee, for that eager heart's annoy?
Misunderstanding, disappointment, tears,
Wronged love, spoiled hope, mistrust and ageing fears,
Eternal longing for one perfect friend,

And unavailing wishes without end?
Thou proud and pure of spirit, how must thou bear
To have thine infinite hates and loves confined,
Schooled, and despised? How keep unquenched and free
'Mid others' commerce and economy
Such ample visions, oft in alien air
Tamed to the measure of the common kind?
How hard for thee, swept on, for ever hurled
From hour to hour, bewildered and forlorn,
To move with clear eyes and with steps secure,
To keep the light within, to fitly scorn
Those all too possible and easy goals,
Trivial ambitions of soon-sated souls!
And, patient in thy purpose, to endure
The pity and the wisdom of the world.

Vain, vain such warning to those happy ears!
Disturb not their delight! By unkind powers
Doomed to keep pace with the relentless Hours,
He, too, ere long, shall feel Earth's glory change;
Familiar names shall take an accent strange,
A deeper meaning, a more human tone;

No more passed by, unheeded or unknown,
The things that then shall be beheld through tears.

Yet, O just Nature, thou
Who, if men's hearts be hard, art always mild;
O fields and streams, and places undefiled,
Let your sweet airs be ever on his brow,
Remember still your child.
Thou too, O human world, if old desires,
If thoughts, not alien once, can move thee now,
Teach him not yet that idly he aspires
Where thou hast failed; not soon let it be plain,
That all who seek in thee for nobler fires,
For generous passion, spend their hopes in vain:
Lest that insidious Fate, foe of mankind,
Who ever waits upon our weakness, try
With whispers his unnerved and faltering mind,
Palsy his powers; for she has spells to dry,
Like the March blast, his blood, turn flesh to stone,
And, conjuring action with necessity,
Freeze the quick will, and make him all her own.

Come, then, as ever, like the Wind at morning!
Joyous, O Youth, in the aged world renew

Freshness to feel the eternities around it,
Rain, stars, and clouds, light and the sacred dew.
The strong sun shines above thee:
That strength, that radiance bring!
If Winter come to Winter,
When shall men hope for Spring?

X.

TO A SOLITARY FIR-TREE.

FIR, that on this moor austere,
Without kin or neighbour near,
Utterest now bleak winter's moan
As if its vext soul were thine own!
Unbefriended, placed like thee,
Ah, how lonely should I be!
But luminous midsummer nights,
Faintly filled with starry lights,
Morns miraculously clear
In the soft youth of the year,
Autumn mists and evenings chill,
Find thee proudly patient still:
None can mar thy steadfast mood,
Thy stanch and stately fortitude.
Had I no heart, to strive, to crave,
I too, perchance, could be as brave!

But oh, to crave and not be filled,
With passionate longing never stilled,
Desiring in the midst of bliss,
Thou, strong Tree, thou know'st not this :
The outstretched arms, the hungry eyes,
Gazing up to silent skies,
Beautiful, silent skies of June,
And radiant mystery of the moon !
To buy peace, we men forget :
But peace is in thy fibres set.
If thou art not stirred with joy,
Thou hast nothing that can cloy;
Without effort, without strife,
Art thyself, and liv'st thy life.
This solitude thou hast not known,
Both to be human and alone.

XI.

PRESENT AND FUTURE.

Look, as a mother bending o'er her boy,
The sleeping boy that in her bosom lies,
Gazes upon him in a trance of joy
With earnest, infinitely tender eyes,
Lost in her deep love, and aware of nought,
Earth and the sunlight, men and trees and skies
Quite faded out from her impassioned thought;
Yet knows one day it will be otherwise,
When, laid alone within the narrow tomb,
Death leaves her none to love; but in youth's bloom,
Or grown to manhood and to strength, her son
Over the same earth that has closed on her
Rejoicing wanders on,
And strikes fresh tracks of thronged and fruitful life,
Nor frets at the sweet need for change and strife,
With eager mind and glowing heart astir

In ardour ever to pursue
Passions and actions, and adventures new :

So is the Present Age,
So strives she for that Age to come, her child,
Which knows not yet the pain, the sacrifice,
She for its sake endures ; it knows not yet,
But must one day, the battles it must wage.
And she, if it within its sleep have smiled,
Is happy in her woes : no vain regret
Saps the sad strength with which she labours still
For that imagined bliss she shall not see,
So dear, so deeply hoped for though it be.
And ever with unconquerable will,
Bearing her burden, toward one distant star
She moves in her desire ; and though with pain
She labour, and the goal she dreams be far,
Proud is she in her passionate soul to know
That from her tears, her very sorrows grow
The joy, the hope, the peace of future men.

XII.

ON A FIGURE OF JUSTICE WITH BOUND EYES.

UNHAPPY goddess!   Has then envious earth
Denied thine eyes the radiance of thy birth?
Have mortals, that still need thy voice to school
Their wrangling lives, their daily feuds to rule,
That thou might'st judge with stern and equal mind,
Swayed by no fear or favour, made thee blind?
Immortal, yet with bound and vacant eye,
How sad an emblem of humanity!
Thou bearest the poised scales, the uplifted sword,
Dealing to each his sentence and award.
Infinite acts in tedious array,
Their petty quarrels, at thy feet they lay.
Thou hearest: and dost thou require no more,
No subtler knowledge, no profounder lore?
Hast thou searched out the individual heart?
Or deem'st thou each its fellow's counterpart?

Ah, what wronged mind might not those eyes have read,
With light and with compassion visited,
Let the soiled page of obscure lots unroll,
Nor from deeds judged, but from the striving soul !

Teased by such strife, and yet, 'mid all its din,
Conscious and proud of heavenly rays within,
Know'st thou no hour when thy long labours seem
Fruitless as foolish, a preposterous dream !
When some imperious impulse bids thee scorn
The bonds of use, no longer to be borne,
And with indignant tears at tasks so vain,
Dash down thy scales, and snap thy sword in twain;
Leave man to end his wrongs from his own store
Of wisdom, and revisit earth no more ?

XIII.

Sweet after labour, soft and whispering night
Blows on dark fields and fragrant country here:
Here there is sleep, to weary limbs delight;
The world is far away, the stars are near.

The world is far away: but there, I know,
Night comes to few unanxious, happy eyes;
And cities, with their restless streets aglow,
Lamps upon lamps, outface the enkindled skies.

London lies there; an endless fiery maze,
Thronged with her millions, sleepless, vast, alone;
The stars are pale above her, where her gaze
Lights the wide heavens and makes the night her own.

There the hot wind blows over no dark fields:
Brief, hard-won rest despotic labours give:
Sleep, to how many spent-out spirits, yields
Life's only sweetness, to forget they live!

XIV.

O SUMMER sun, O moving trees !
O cheerful human noise, O busy glittering street !
What hour shall Fate in all the future find,
Or what delights, ever to equal these :
Only to taste the warmth, the light, the wind,
Only to be alive, and feel that life is sweet ?

D

XV.

DISAPPOINTMENT.

AND were they but for this, those passionate schemes
  Of joy, that I have nursed? indeed for this
That longings, day and night, have filled my dreams?
  Now it has come, the hour of bliss,
    How different it seems!

So thought I bitterly: but on my bed
  As I lay lone and restless, in my ear,
Falling from some far place of peace o'erhead
  Through the still dark, I seemed to hear
    These accents softly shed:

"Wouldst thou then, child, from this invading pain
  Find refuge, and relax thy suffering will
In tears? To peace wouldst thou indeed attain?
  Remember all thy courage; still
    True to thyself remain!

" What is it to thee, if some wished delight,
    That from the future beckoned thee, at last
Comes changed, its former glory faded quite?
    Fly the perfidious Hours; keep fast
        Within, the springs of light!

" What is it to thee, if in some dear mind
    Another is remembered, more than thou?
Quench that poor envy; let no gazer find
    Aught in thine acts or on thy brow
        But what is sweet and kind!

" For how shall that pure spirit, whom vain things flee,
    Whom passion's ebbs and floods delight not, Love
The consolation of the world, if he
    Out of his course so lightly move,
        Immortal and eternal be?

" Take courage! peace at last and joy attend
    The true-fixt heart that mocks Time's envious power;
The heart that, tender even to the end,
    Exacts not joy from any hour,
        Nor love from any friend."

Alas ! how oft I have wished that voice had spared
  Its counsel stern, nor pointed me through tears
My path !   How oft, to feet stumbling and scarred,
  That path impossible appears;
    Which yet is only hard.

XVI.

AMO, ERGO SUM.

WHATEVER seemed to reign within my breast,
Ere now, or reigned in the true sovereign's room,
Love has dethroned, strong Love has dispossessed,
Like a glad master come to his own home.
     Love is my lord: I call upon his name.

Aimless I lived; but now my aims are flown
Winged to one mark, wherever his voice call:
My heart shrinks from deep pains, too well foreknown,
But my soul leaps with joy, to welcome all.
     With Love, my joy, I have no fear of shame.

So that Love lead my ever-faithful feet,
I care not whether they be scarred or no.
Somehow, somewhere, the end must needs be sweet,
However rough the road by which we go.
     Love is my trust; for since I love, I am.

XVII.

NAME, that makes my heart beat,
Heard by chance in the thronged street,
How delighted I turn to greet
The vision adored, the vision rare,
  That surely should be where thou art spoken!

Alas, alas! it is not there:
Only hurrying faces stare,
Hard faces, in cold surprise,
Amazed at the joy that out of my eyes
Shines expectant, and then dies
  Disappointed, the sweet spell broken!

XVIII.

O WORLD, be nobler, for her sake!
  If she but knew thee, what thou art,
  What wrongs are borne, what deeds are done
  In thee, beneath thy daily sun,
  Know'st thou not that her tender heart,
For pain and very shame, would break?
O World, be nobler, for her sake!

XIX.

RECOLLECTIONS OF CORNWALL.

To R. G. R. and H. P. P.

Let not the mind, that would have peace,
Too much repose on former joy,
Nor in pourtraying past delight
Her needed, active power employ!

So, as we linger and look back,
Tired, and perplext with present fears,
Comes the clear voice of something stern
Across the frivolous, fleeting years.

Pressed onward, without power to pause,
By their imperious, silent wave,
How little of the precious past,
Hoarded so anxiously, we save.

Scarce with beseeching tears we cry,
To some delicious moment, stay !
Ere the rude hours have swept us on :
Lamenting we are borne away.

Yet often, in our deep desire,
Backward we cannot help but gaze,
If gazing might perchance restore
Some lost and lovely yesterdays.

Come then, and ere Time takes them quite,
Gather with careful choice, to find
Whatever flowering memories serve
To make a garden of the mind.

Near tender thoughts and unsoiled names,
Names murmured to our hearts in sleep,
And dreams, too pure for the world's eye,
These too, their sacred place shall keep.

Then let the cloud-swept midnight blow
Fresh on our cheeks again the spray,
As the prow plunges, where we stand
And watch the coast, from bay to bay.

Lying so lonely, sleeping soft
Under the breezes of the night;
Only on each dim headland gleams,
Far-seen, its beaconing, faithful light.

Again upon our waking eyes
Let Plymouth Sound and Plymouth Hoe,
The woody Mount, the ships, the strand,
Bright in the morning sunshine glow.

Or let the tender twilight steep,
As at our journey's end, the moor,
When glad and tired at last we reach
The Lizard, and our cottage door.

The Lizard! hark! the name brings back
The noise remote of moving seas,
Storied as those, whose waters foamed
Round the renowned Hesperides.

On Kynance Cove our window looks,
The foam-swept rocks, the tides' unrest,
The gathering dusk, and one pure star
Deep in the visionary west.

And there we sit, while evening dies
Far o'er that lone, romantic sea,
Where famous, fallen Lyonness
Sleeps with its ruined chivalry.

By Dolour Hugo's wondrous walls,
Under their arching gloom we glide :
Rocking our boat, with rustling noise,
The shadowy waters swell, subside.

Cold strikes the air; our voices wake
Weird echoes in the roof: below,
Deep through the glimmering waves, we see
The long weeds washing to and fro.

Then round the headland's troops of gulls
To hospitable Cadgwith come;
Sweet Cadgwith, climbing o'er the cliff
With cottage gardens bright in bloom.

Ah, morns at Housel, where we bathe !
Where, sounding up the cliffs and caves,
The blue sea tumbles, salt and bright;
Fresh in our faces burst the waves.

Ah, that wild slope, beyond Penzance,
Where, deep in heather, drowsed we lie,
Till on us steals the fairy mist
And makes a blank of sea and sky;

Blots out the distant Lizard coast,
And steals across the silent bay:
Saint Michael's Mount becomes a cloud,
And dimly wanes the lingering day.

So may not the oblivious months
With other scenes, however bright,
Wash out your names, with all that made
Our sojourn by your shores delight.

Sweet shores! to the remembering mind
Thrice lovelier now: for what were ye
Without the charm, that still survives,
Of chosen friends' society?

Nay, can Earth's sweetest sights and sounds,
A running stream, a rosy sky,
Uncheered by human thoughts, assuage
The deep desire for sympathy?

Like a fair face, without a heart,
They charm, and for an hour control ;
But easily we turn away :
They have not lingered in the soul.

XX.

KENNACK SANDS.

On Kennack Sands the sun
Shines, and the fresh wind blows,
Moulding pale banks anew,
Where the sea-holly grows.
Waters softly blue
And exquisitely clear
Meet the o'er-arching sky;
O'er them the breezes run.
There may'st thou idly lie,
And still find new delights,
Watching the gulls' white flights
Above that lonely place;
Listen, nor ever hear
A single human sound
To spoil the free, profound,
Aerial quietness.

But when thou'rt gone, the night
On Kennack comes; and soon,
Lovely beyond dreams,
Arises the round moon;
In whose trembling light
The rough splendour gleams
Of the crested sea.
Ah, could'st thou there then be!
But mortal ears can hear not
What those pale sands hear then;
Sounds not of mortal birth,
Laughter, and dance, and mirth,
Of the golden-haired sea-fairies,
Mermaidens and mermen.

XXI.

THE AUTUMN CROCUS.

In the high woods that crest our hills,
Upon a steep, rough slope of forest ground,
Where few flowers grow, sweet blooms to-day I found
Of the Autumn Crocus, blowing pale and fair.
           Dim falls the sunlight there;
And a mild fragrance the lone thicket fills.

    Languidly curved, the long white stems
Their purple flowers' gold treasure scarce display :
Lost were their leaves since, in the distant spring,
Their February sisters showed so gay.
Roses of June, ye too have followed fleet !
Forsaken now, and shaded as by thought,
As by the human shade of thought and dreams,
They bloom 'mid the dark wood, whose air has wrought

With what soft nights and mornings of still dew !
Into their slender petals that clear hue,
    Like paleness in fresh cheeks ; a thing
      On earth, I vowed, ne'er grew
More delicately pure, more shyly sweet.

    Child of the pensive autumn woods !
So lovely, though thou dwell obscure and lone.
And though thy flush and gaiety be gone ;
Say, among flowers of the sad, human mind,
      Where shall I ever find
So rare a grace ? in what shy solitudes ?

XXII.

STARS.

AND must I deem you mortal as my kind,
O solemn stars, that to man's doubtful mind
So long have seemed, 'mid the world's fallen kings
And glories gone, the sole eternal things;
To perishable flesh and mouldering dust
Heaven's symbols fixt, triumphant and august?
Do ye too suffer change, ye too decay,
Waxing and waning like an earthly day?
So must I deem: yet not with such a light
Shine ye, on this serene September night!
No, nor as alien splendours, worlds not ours,
In perfect order marshalled, mighty Powers,
Beneath whose peace we darkly do and dream:
Not now so vast, not so remote ye seem.
But, it may be some rising human tear
That dims my eyes and draws your radiance near,

Sweet tokens of the lands ye look upon,
Faces upturned like mine, unknown yet known,
Of musing friends and lovers, ye appear !
Pulses of Heaven, whose beating mirrors forth
The beating of the unnumbered hearts of earth !
Eyes, that in love watch over weary men !
Once more I lift my gaze to you, as then
In childhood, when you seemed but lovely lights,
The glorious visitants of cloudless nights ;
And, as I gaze, I feel renewed the joy
Ignorance felt, nor knowledge can destroy.

XXIII.

PINE TREES.

Down through the heart of the dim woods
The laden, jolting waggons come.
Tall pines, chained together,
They carry; stems straight and bare,
Now no more in their own solitudes
With proud heads to rock and hum;
Now at the will of men to fare
Away from their brethren, their forest friends
In the still woods; through wild weather
Alone to endure to the world's ends:
Soon to feel the power of the North
Careering over dark waves' foam;
Soon to exchange for the steady earth
Heaving decks; for the scents of their home,
Honeyed wild-thyme, gorse, and heather,
The sting of the spray, the bitter air.

XXIV.

TWILIGHT.

WARM, the deserted evening
  Closes over the moor.
Was it here we walked and were merry
  Only an hour before?

Magic light in the west
  Smiles over the moorland swells:
Fairies invisible roam them
  Whispering wonderful spells.

They whisper, and all grows strange:
  Shadows are over the stream;
The still, gray rocks are a vision,
  The solid ground a dream.

Trees murmur, and hush, and tremble;
  The west is drained of light.
Earth slumbers beneath silence
  And the beautiful eyes of Night.

XXV.

Now that I have won
    Long despaired of peace,
And those fears are flown
    That vext so my heart's ease;

Shall I wish my love
    Had found a path more smooth,
With no thorns to prove
    Its constancy and truth ?

Wish those nights not spent,
    Long, unhappy nights,
Which in sighings went
    Over lost delights ?

Wish those tears unwept,
    When you seemed unkind ?
Nay; for these pangs kept
    Love steadfast in my mind.

Out of these he came
  Stronger, tenderer; tried
As with burning flame;
  Proved and purified.

Not in vain I shook
  With those tears and sighs,
If now Love may look
  Out of Faith's clear eyes.

Now may my tired head
  On your breast repose,
By your heart comforted,
  Which it trusts and knows.

XXVI.

No more now with jealous complaining
Shall you be vext; nor I with fears
Torture my heart: my heart is secure now,
And laughs at follies of former tears.
No more now with the endless paining
Of idle desires shall Day distress;
Nor Night, from passionate envy pure now,
With insupportable loneliness.
Truth and Trust so sweetly possess
My fortress of peace, no more to be shaken;
From dreams of joy to joy I awaken
And wander in fields of happiness.
Foolish once, now I'll be wise,
And live in the light of your trusting eyes.

XXVII

MIDSUMMER VIGIL.

NIGHT smiles on me with her stars,
Mystic, pure, enchanted, lone.
Light, that only heaven discloses,
Is in heaven that no cloud mars;
Here, through murmuring darkness blown,
Comes the scent of unseen roses.

Now the world is all asleep;
Drowsy man dull rest is taking.
I with whispering trees apart
My deserted vigil keep.
Light leaves in the light wind shaking
Echo back my beating heart.

And the garden's perfumes thrill me
Like a touch or whispered name :
Heliotrope and lavender
Slumber-odoured lilies, fill me

With their breath, like subtlest flame;
Vague desire and yearning stir.

Shadowy elms above me, crowned
With mysterious foliage, dim
Mid the stars, against the skies,
Hidden lawn and alley bound,
Full of voices, full of dream,
Fragrant breathings and long sighs.

Wishes, that with eager tongues
Strive among the soft-blown boughs,
Each an amorous messenger;
Dreams, that glide in noiseless throngs;
Wingèd flight of earnest vows;
Listening with hushed breath I hear.

This intoxicating sweetness
That the perfumed air exhales,
Stir of thoughts and dear desires,
Joys that faint with their own fleetness,
Passion that for utterance fails;
Whither burns it? where aspires?

'Tis for her, whose worshipped hand
Holds my heart, for life, for death.
Ah, could she, could she but come
Hither, where Love's witching wand
Holds the midnight's thoughtful breath,
While the stars are glittering dumb!

Come, that into that sweet ear
I might pour what until now
Never heart brought tongue to tell,
Mistress ne'er had bliss to hear,
Lover with his hundredth vow
Vainly sought to syllable.

Pale with transport when I take
'Twixt my hands her face, and look
Deep into her brimming eyes,
Passionately fain to speak,
How my trembling murmurs mock
Those unuttered ecstacies!

And when cheek to cheek is prest,
And the pulse of her pure being

Throbs from her veins into mine,
Love in torment from my breast
Cries athirst for language, freeing
In sweet speech his pangs divine.

How should language, weak and vain,
Bear the burden of such joy?
How should words the meaning reach
Of that charm's ecstatic pain;
Charm which words would but destroy
Of devotion beyond speech?

But to-night, dear, Love is kind,
And those jealous bonds that mesh
The heart's tongue-tied truth sets free.
Undivided, unconfined
By those walls of human flesh,
Look, my heart is bared to thee!

Seeing, thou shalt want not eyes;
Hearing, thou shalt need not ears;
Purged, our spirits shall burn through
Tedious day's necessities.

O to cast off doubts and fears !
To touch truth, and feel it true !

Thou my tender thought shalt find
Ever, like a quick-eyed slave,
Watching for thy wish unspoken ;
In my inmost treasury shrined
Looks and tones thy spirit gave,
Faith's for ever cherished token!

Come, O come, where'er thou art !
Ere this rich hour past reprieve
In the garish daylight die,
Hear me, Sweet, and my heart's heart,
My soul's soul, believe, receive,
Poured into a single sigh !

XXVIII.

Ask me not, Dear, what thing it is
 That makes me love you so ;
What graces, what sweet qualities,
 That from your spirit flow :
For I have but this old reply,
That you are you, that I am I.

My heart leaps when you look on me,
 And thrills to hear your voice.
Lies, then, in these the mystery
 That makes my soul rejoice ?
I only know, I love you true ;
Since I am I, and you are you.

XXIX.

CHERWELL STREAM.

GREEN banks and gliding river !
    What air from what far place
    Comes down your waters' face
And makes your willows shiver ?

Over me stole a spell,
A breath upon my brow ;
Light on my spirit fell,
I knew not whence nor how.

Faded into a dream
Are Oxford's spires and towers ;
Far down the winding stream,
Beyond the fields and flowers.

Is it that Nature here,
Finding me thus alone,
Would whisper in my ear
Some secret of her own ?

Would win her child again
To these beloved retreats,
Shunned now too long for men,
For throngs and busy streets?

I know not.   Round the bend
    The sound of oars comes fast:
    My moment's spell is past;
I hear the voice of a friend.

XXX.

TINTAGEL.

Low is laid Arthur's head,
  Unknown earth above him mounded;
By him sleep his splendid knights,
  With whose names the world resounded.
Ruined glories! flown delights,
  Sunk 'mid rumours of old wars!
Where they revelled, deep they sleep
  By the wild Atlantic shores.

On Tintagel's fortressed walls,
  Proudly built, the loud sea scorning,
Pale the moving moonlight falls;
  Through their rents the wind goes mourning.
See ye, Knights, your ancient home,
  Chafed and spoiled and fallen asunder?
Hear ye now, as then of old,
  Waters rolled, and wrath of foam,
Where the waves beneath your graves
  Snow themselves abroad in thunder?

F

XXXI.

Ah, now this happy month is gone,
Not now, my heart, complain,
Nor rail at Time because so soon
He takes his own again.

He takes his own, the weeks, the hours,
But leaves the best with thee;
Seeds of imperishable flowers
In fields of memory.

XXXII.

Do kings put faith in fortressed walls, and bar
Their cities' gates, as strong to keep out war?
   The constancy of friends is stronger far.
Are lilies pure, that in some vale unknown
Unplucked have blossomed and unpraised have blown?
   The constancy of friends is purer.
The constancy of friends is lovelier
Than fame or fortune; past all riches dear;
Impossible to soil by foulest breath;
Their crown is rarer than the conqueror's wreath,
   And all their joy securer.

Then let our love be simple, steadfast, true,
And we will Fate and all her arms defy.
With that blind conflict what have we to do,
However stabbed at by Adversity?
The mortal foe is slain, mistrust; the dread
Lest our love lean upon uncertainty;

F—2

Mistrust, that poisons the mind's daily bread,
And kills its needful faith.
For us, since our joined hands have made us brave,
           Not ev'n Love's boastful foes,
Estranging Time nor separating Death,
           Shall call us slave,
So that we keep perfect the name of those
Who did not buy each other's hearts, but gave.

XXXIII.

O sorrowful thought ! But one more flying year,
And our ways part, perhaps no more to meet :
        And must we, then, less dear
Grow to each other, as the swift days fleet ?

Look, as two boughs from one stem branching grow
Apart, until their high leaves touch no longer ;
        Save when some chance gust, stronger
Than most, the one back to the other blow :

Like that tree's branches, so shall we two be ;
Our paths how far divorced from where they started !
        Yet still, however parted,
Rooted in the dear past and memory.

Time cannot take those; for our souls are free,
Whatever come. Then O when you have leisure
        For old thoughts, think of me,
Whose mind holds you for its most treasured treasure.

XXXIV.

VISION of peace, Joy without stain,
    That on my vext heart sweetly shinest,
Hast thou, too, known the touch of pain,
Cares and dark hours, when in vain
    For thy lost quiet thou repinest?

Have those eyes, in whose pure spheres
    A refuge seems for all annoy,
Been indeed the place of tears?
Ah! grieve with those whom grief endears:
    Still, still to me be only Joy!

XXXV.

FORTUNATE MOMENTS.

Hast thou not known them, too, these moments
    bright,
Rare moments, such as came to me but now,
On this clear, breezy evening, when the light
Flows through the orchard's tossing leaf and bough,
As though beyond their lifted screen the breeze
Would open magic visions of the Hesperides?

Hast thou not felt a strange, arresting sense
Charm thee with wonder, fill thee unaware;
A sense of something, come thou know'st not whence,
Invisible new beauty in the air,
Wings in the light, or glory in the wind,
Make the heart throb, illumine the enchanted mind?

Ah, what an exaltation of the breast!
Ah, what a radiant clearness of the brain!
Easy it seems to find and choose the best;
Thou know'st what thou must do, the path is plain;
And read'st the riddles that beset thy soul;
While to purged eyes the mysteries of the world unroll.

But O what quick relapse! the moment come
Unrealised departs: 'tis faded quite.
Only the garden greets thee of thy home;
Only the green trees wave in the still light.
Again with puzzling brow thou stand'st alone,
With the remembered dream of light and glory gone.

XXXVI.

I HAVE too happy been.
Some sad Fate envies me.
An arrow she, unseen,
Has fitted to her bow,
And smiling grim, I know,
Let the drawn shaft leap free.

Deep in my side it pierced:
With sudden pain I shook,
And gazed around, the accurst
Perfidious foe to espy.
Lo, only thou art nigh,
With sweet and troubled look!

XXXVII.

WHAT shall I say to thee, my spirit, so soon dejected,
    Unaccountably conquered, where thou seemed'st
        strong ?
Life, that, yesterday, the sun's own glory reflected,
    Darkened now, like a train of captives, crawls along.

Alas ! 'tis an old trouble, vainly drugged to sleep.
    Let it wake outright; be proved, confronted, known.
Desire however endless, love however deep
    Still must search and hunger : thou art still alone.

Alone, alone ! Ah, little avails with childish tears
    In the night's silent darkness to struggle against thy
        pain ;
With hands stretched out in a prayer that seems to reach
        no ears,
    And desolate repetition of that forlorn refrain.

Alone into the world thou camest, and wast not afraid.
   Out of it must thou go, with no hand to clasp thine.
Thou fear'st not death: why now need'st thou another's
      aid
   To live thine own life out, nor falter and repine?

XXXVIII.

Come back, sweet yesterdays!
Sweet yesterdays, come back!
Ah! not in my dreams only
Vex me with joy, to wake
From dream to truth, twice lonely,
And with renewed heart-ache.
Let night be wholly black,
So day have some kind rays.
Come back, sweet yesterdays!
Sweet yesterdays, come back!

XXXIX.

Go now, Love,
   Since staying's joy no longer!
Leave me to prove
   If Time can make me stronger!
Nay, look not over thy shoulder so,
Pleading so sweetly to remain,
Where thou workest so much pain :
Look not behind thee, haste and go!

Ah, how should I
   Deal to thee such hard measure,
As force thee fly,
   Who brought me heavenly pleasure?
Take pity, Love, and be kind
To him that could not refuse thee!
Is it not grief enough to lose thee?
Haste, O haste, nor look behind!

XL

How dark, how quiet sleeps the vale below!
In the dim farms, look, not a window shines:
Distantly heard among the lonely pines,
How soft the languid autumn breezes flow
Past me, and kiss my hair, and cheek, and mouth!
> Half-veiled is the calm sky:
> Jupiter's kingly eye
Alone glows full in the unclouded South.

Alas! and can sweet Night avail to heal
Not one of the world's wounds? Must I, even here,
Still listen with the mind's too wakeful ear
To that sad sound, which in my flesh I feel;
Sound of unresting, unrejoicing feet,
> With feverish steps or slow
> For ever, to and fro,
Pacing the gay, thronged, friendless, stony street?

Nature is free; but Man the eternal slave
Of care and passion. Must I deem that true?

With fields and quiet have we nought to do,
Because our spirits for ever crave and crave,
And never found their satisfaction yet ? ˙
        World, is thy heart so cold,
        So deeply weary and old,
That thy sole business is but to forget ?

No, no ! these perfect trees, with whispering voice,
These flowers, that have to thee a solace been,
And yet an alien solace, so serene
They live, and in their life seem to rejoice ;
Life how unlike to thine ! These flowers, these trees,
        Are children of one birth
        With thee, O Man ; as Earth,
Earth, still so fair, for all thy ravages,

Is sister to yon radiant Jupiter,
Who with such glorious and untroubled gaze
Upon his own course burning down Heaven's ways
Across deep seas of darkness looks at her !
Perchance in his vast bosom he, too, keeps
        Like ferment, like distress ;
        Yet tranquil shines not less,
Lord of the night, that round his splendour sleeps.

XLI.

THE LAST EVENING.

OVER sea the sun in a mystery of light
Burns across the waters, on the blown spray glancing:
Luminously crested, wave behind wave advancing
Pours its rushing foam with low continual roar.
The wide sands around us, flashing wet and bright,
Mirror cliffs suffused with clearest warmth serene,
Rosy earth, gray rocks, and grass of greenest green;
We two pace together the solitary shore.

A sadness and a joy are mingled in the air.
From the dying day a voice, *I go and come back never*,
From the waves an answering shout, *We rush, we break
    for ever*,
Wake in my heart echoes that conflicting swell.
Now on the last evening, now we are aware
Of something in our souls that will not say, 'Tis ended.
In our parting looks are thoughts eternal blended:
See, our hands are joined; we cannot say farewell!

XLII.

O CRUDELIS AMOR!

It was Spring, the sweet Spring, when first I met with
    Love.
  Suddenly I raised my eyes; and he stood there.
He was so beautiful, I could not look elsewhere.
  For joy I could not speak; I gazed, but could not
    move;
  But all my body trembled, as he spoke and stole,
  With his voice's wonder, my surrendered soul.
Ah, why was there none nigh, to whisper me, *Beware?*

G

XLIII.

As I walked through London,
The fresh wound burning in my breast,
As I walked through London,
Longing to have forgotten, to harden my heart, and to
     rest,
A sudden consolation, a softening light
Touched me: the streets alive and bright,
With hundreds each way thronging, on their tide
Received me, a drop in the stream, unmarked, unknown.
And to my heart I cried:
Here can thy trouble find shelter, thy wound be eased!
For see, not thou alone,
But thousands, each with his smart,
Deep-hidden, perchance, but felt in the core of the heart!
And as to a sick man's feverish veins
The full sponge warmly pressed,

Relieves with its burning the burning of forehead and
    hands,
So, I, to my aching breast,
Gathered the griefs of those thousands, and made them
    my own ;
My bitterest pains
Merged in a tenderer sorrow, assuaged and appeased.

XLIV.

Dear child, thou know'st, I blame not thee;
Thou too, I know, hast shared my smart.
Neither did wrong; 'twas only she,
Nature, that moulded us apart.

But not to have sinned, in Nature's eyes,
I find a brittle plea to trust:
She punishes the just unwise
More hardly than the wise unjust.

She placed our souls, like Heaven's lone spheres,
In separate paths, no power can move:
O truth too heart-breaking for tears!
Not even Love, not even Love!

XLV.

STERN Power, whose heavy hand I feel,
Whose infinite, world-urging force,
Nor silent pain nor strong appeal
Persuades from its imperious course,

Idly I strive with thee; 'tis thou
Rul'st in this world of thwarted will!
To thine omnipotence I bow;
And dare to disobey thee still.

XLVI.

THE shrines of old are broken down;
The faiths that knelt at them are dead.
Nothing's strange, and nought unknown :
All's been done and all been said.
Tired of knowledge, now we sigh
For a little mystery.

Yet, howsoever science delves,
A few things still unplumbed remain.
We know all things save ourselves,
Cannot will our joy or pain.
Mysteries our hearts enthral ;
And love's the strangest of them all.

XLVII.

BEAUTIFULLY dies the year.
Silence sleeps upon the mere :
Yellow leaves float on it, stilly
As, in June, the opened lily.
Brushing o'er the frosty grass
I watch a moment, ere I pass,
From beeches that will soon be bare
Down the still November air
The lovely ways of gliding leaves.
Perhaps they budded on Spring eves
When we two walked and talked together !
Autumn thoughts for Autumn weather !
I wish some days that I remember
Could glide from me, this fair November.

XLVIII.

The sun goes down, on other lands to shine.
I long to keep him, but he will not stay.
Only in fancy can I wing my way
To overtake him, to recatch each ray,
Warmer and warmer, till at last is mine,
In fancy, that loved gaze, that light divine.

Now close the dewy flowers, that morn's first peep
To sunshine opened : and I too must close
My leaves up, and in silence and repose
Baptize my spirit. See, the last gleam goes :
Now is it time neither to joy nor weep ;
Only to lay the head down, and to sleep.

XLIX.

THE VICTORIA, LOST OFF TRIPOLI,

JUNE, 1893.

HEROES, whose days are told,
　Above whose bodies brave
Presses the heavy, cold,
　　And quenching wave!

Ye sleep: but your bright fame,
　Blown upon every breeze,
Touches with mournful flame
　　The Syrian seas.

Now all your English land
　Trembles with tears, with pride;
Stretching toward you her hand,
　　O glorified!

H

There he that walks alone,
A vision goes with him;
In still field or thronged town,
A solemn dream!

He sees the placid, blue
Mediterranean shine;
The warships, two and two,
In ordered line.

He sees those consorts vast
On their doomed circle come.
With held breath, and aghast,
The Fleet is dumb.

For him the moments hang;
His ears the shock await:
On him, too, a strong pang
Fastens, like fate.

Transfixt, his eyes see then
The decks heave, lined with free,
Firm ranks; weaponless men,
Matched with the Sea.

Alas ! the wound is deep.
  Not even spirits so brave
Their vainly splendid ship
  Keep from the wave.

On their last farewell cries
  Shines the permitting sun ;
With his men Tryon lies ;
  And all is done.

Yet through some hearts the prayer
  Thrills, O that I had died,
Fallen in glory there
  By comrades' side !

Printed by R. Folkard & Son,
22, Devonshire St., Queen Sq., London.

List of Books

in

Belles Lettres

ALL THE BOOKS IN THIS CATALOGUE ARE
PUBLISHED AT NET PRICES.

1894

Telegraphic Address—
'BODLEIAN, LONDON.'

'A WORD must be said for the manner in which the publishers have produced the volume (*i.e.*, "The Earth Fiend"), a sumptuous folio, printed by CONSTABLE, the etchings on Japanese paper by MR. GOULDING. The volume should add not only to MR. STRANG's fame but to that of MESSRS. ELKIN MATHEWS AND JOHN LANE, who are rapidly gaining distinction for their beautiful editions of belles-lettres.'—*Daily Chronicle*, Sept. 24, 1892.

Referring to MR. LE GALLIENNE'S 'English Poems' and 'Silhouettes' by MR. ARTHUR SYMONS:—'We only refer to them now to note a fact which they illustrate, and which we have been observing of late, namely, the recovery to a certain extent of good taste in the matter of printing and binding books These two books, which are turned out by MESSRS. ELKIN MATHEWS AND JOHN LANE, are models of artistic publishing, and yet they are simplicity itself. The books with their excellent printing and their very simplicity make a harmony which is satisfying to the artistic sense.'—*Sunday Sun*, Oct. 2, 1892.

'MR. LE GALLIENNE is a fortunate young gentleman. I don't know by what legerdemain he and his publishers work, but here, in an age as stony to poetry as the ages of Chatterton and Richard Savage, we find the full edition of his book sold before publication. How is it done, MESSRS. ELKIN MATHEWS AND JOHN LANE? for, without depreciating MR. LE GALLIENNE'S sweetness and charm, I doubt that the marvel would have been wrought under another publisher. These publishers, indeed, produce books so delightfully, that it must give an added pleasure to the hoarding of first editions.'—KATHARINE TYNAN in *The Irish Daily Independent*.

'To MESSRS. ELKIN MATHEWS AND JOHN LANE almost more than to any other, we take it, are the thanks of the grateful singer especially due; for it is they who have managed, by means of limited editions and charming workmanship, to impress book-buyers with the belief that a volume may have an æsthetic and commercial value. They have made it possible to speculate in the latest discovered poet, as in a new company—with the difference that an operation in the former can be done with three half-crowns.'—*St. James's Gazette*.

January, 1894.

List of Books

IN

BELLES LETTRES

(Including some Transfers)

PUBLISHED BY

Elkin Mathews & John Lane

The Bodley Head

VIGO STREET, LONDON, W.

N.B.—The Authors and Publishers reserve the right of reprinting any book in this list if a new Edition is called for, except in cases where a stipulation has been made to the contrary, and of printing a separate edition of any of the books for America irrespective of the numbers to which the English editions are limited. The numbers mentioned do not include the copies sent for review, nor those supplied to the public libraries.

➤§§➤

ADAMS (FRANCIS).

    ESSAYS IN MODERNITY. cr. 8vo. 5s. *net.*

                             [*In preparation.*

ALLEN (GRANT).

    THE LOWER SLOPES: A VOLUME OF VERSE, with title page and cover design by J. ILLINGWORTH KAY. 600 copies, cr. 8vo. 5s. *net.*   [*Immediately.*

ANTÆUS.

    THE BACKSLIDER, AND OTHER POEMS. 100 only, sm. 4to. 7s. 6d. *net.*   [*Very few remain.*

BEECHING (H. C.), J. W. MACKAIL, and
    J. B. B. NICHOLS.
    LOVE IN IDLENESS, with Vignette by W. B. SCOTT.
        Fcap. 8vo., half vellum.   12s. *net*.   [*Very few remain.*
    Transferred by the Authors to the present publishers.

BENSON (ARTHUR CHRISTOPHER).
    POEMS.   550 copies, fcap. 8vo.   5s. *net*.

BENSON (EUGENE).
    FROM THE ASOLAN HILLS.   A Poem.   300 copies, imp.
        16mo.   5s. *net*.   [*Very few remain.*

BINYON (LAURENCE).
    LYRIC POEMS, with title page by SELWYN IMAGE.   Sq.
        16mo.   5s. *net*.

BOURDILLON (F. W.).
    A LOST GOD.   A Poem, with Illustrations by H. J. FORD.
        500 copies, 8vo.   6s. *net*.   [*Very few remain.*

BOURDILLON (F. W.).
    AILES D'ALOUETTE   Poems printed at the private press
        of Rev. H. DANIEL, Oxford.   100 only, 16mo.
        £1. 10s. *net*.   [*Not published.*

BRIDGES (ROBERT).
    THE GROWTH OF LOVE.   Printed in Fell's Old English
        type at the private press of Rev. H. DANIEL, Oxford.
        100 only, fcap. 4to.   £2. 12s. 6d. *net*.   [*Not published.*

COLERIDGE (HON. STEPHEN).
    THE SANCTITY OF CONFESSION.   A Romance.   2nd edi-
        tion, cr. 8vo.   3s. *net*.   [*A few remain.*

CRANE (WALTER).
    RENASCENCE.   A Book of Verse.   Frontispiece and 38 designs
        by the Author.   [*Small paper edition out of print.*
        There remain a few large paper copies, fcap. 4to.
        £1. 1s. *net*.   And a few fcap. 4to. Japanese vellum.
        £1. 15s. *net*.

CROSSING (WM.)

THE ANCIENT CROSSES OF DARTMOOR. With 11 plates, 8vo. cloth. 4s. 6d. net. [*Very few remain.*

DAVIDSON (JOHN).

PLAYS: An Unhistorical Pastoral; A Romantic Farce; Bruce, a Chronicle Play; Smith, a Tragic Farce; Scaramouch in Naxos, a Pantomime, with a frontispiece and cover design by AUBREY BEARDSLEY. 500 copies. Small 4to. 7s. 6d. net.

DAVIDSON (JOHN).

THE NORTH WALL. Fcap. 8vo. 2s. 6d. net. [*Very few remain. Transferred by the Author to the present Publishers.*

DAVIDSON (JOHN).

FLEET STREET ECLOGUES. 2nd edition, fcap. 8vo. buckram. 5s. net.

DAVIDSON (JOHN).

A RANDOM ITINERARY: Prose Sketches, with a Ballad. Frontispiece, title page, and cover design by LAURENCE HOUSMAN. Fcap. 8vo. 5s. net.

DE GRUCHY (AUGUSTA).

UNDER THE HAWTHORN, AND OTHER VERSES. *Frontispiece by Walter Crane.* 300 copies, cr. 8vo. 5s. net. Also 30 copies on Japanese vellum. 15s. net. [*Very few remain.*

DE TABLEY (LORD).

POEMS, DRAMATIC AND LYRICAL. By JOHN LEICESTER WARREN (Lord De Tabley), illustrations and cover design by C. S. RICKETTS. 2nd edition, cr. 8vo. 7s. 6d. net.

DIAL (THE).

No. 2. Illustrations by RICKETTS, SHANNON, and PISSARO, 200 only, 4to. £1. 1s. net. [*Very few remain. The present series will be continued at irregular intervals.*

EGERTON (GEORGE).

   KEYNOTES.   Short Stories, with title page by AUBREY
      BEARDSLEY.   2nd edition, cr. 8vo.   3s. 6d. net.

FIELD (MICHAEL).

   SIGHT AND SONG (Poems on Pictures).   400 copies, fcap.
      8vo.   5s. net.   [*Very few remain.*

FIELD (MICHAEL).

   STEPHANIA: A TRIALOGUE IN 3 ACTS.   250 copies,
      pott 4to.   6s. net.   [*Very few remain.*

GALE (NORMAN).

   ORCHARD SONGS, with title page and cover design by
      J. ILLINGWORTH KAY.   Fcap. 8vo.   5s. net.
      Also a special edition, limited in number, on hand-made
      paper, bound in English vellum.   £1. 1s. net.

GARNETT (RICHARD).

   POEMS, with title page designed by J. ILLINGWORTH KAY.
      350 copies, cr. 8vo.   5s. net.

GOSSE (EDMUND).

   THE LETTERS OF THOMAS LOVELL BEDDOES.   Now
      first edited.   Pott 8vo.   5s. net.   [*Shortly.*

GRAHAME (KENNETH).

   PAGAN PAPERS: A VOLUME OF ESSAYS, with title page by
      AUBREY BEARDSLEY.   Fcap. 8vo.   5s. net.

GREENE (G. A.).

   ITALIAN LYRISTS OF TO-DAY.   Translations in the origi-
      nal metres from about 35 living Italian poets ; with bibli-
      ographical and biographical notes, cr. 8vo.   5s. net.

HAKE (DR. T. GORDON).

   A SELECTION FROM HIS POEMS.   Edited by Mrs. MEY-
      NELL, with a portrait after D. G. ROSSETTI.   Cr. 8vo.
      5s. net.   [*Shortly.*

HALLAM (ARTHUR HENRY).

THE POEMS, together with his Essay "On some of the Characteristics of Modern Poetry and on the Lyrical Poems of Alfred Tennyson." Edited, with an introduction, by RICHARD LE GALLIENNE, 550 copies, fcap. 8vo. 5s. net. [Very few remain.

HAMILTON (COL. IAN).

THE BALLAD OF HADJI, AND OTHER POEMS. Etched frontispiece by WM. STRANG. 550 copies, fcap. 8vo. 3s. net.

Transferred by the Author to the present Publishers.

HAYES (ALFRED).

THE VALE OF ARDEN, AND OTHER POEMS. With title page and cover design by LAURENCE HOUSMAN. Fcap. 8vo. 5s. net. [In preparation.

HICKEY (EMILY H.).

VERSE TALES, LYRICS, AND TRANSLATIONS. 300 copies, imp. 16mo. 5s. net.

HORNE (HERBERT P.).

DIVERSI COLORES. Poems with ornaments by the Author, 250 copies, 16mo. 5s. net.

IMAGE (SELWYN).

CAROLS AND POEMS, with decorations by H. P. HORNE, 250 copies, 16mo. 5s. net. [In preparation.

JAMES (W. P.).

ROMANTIC PROFESSIONS : A VOLUME OF ESSAYS. With title page by J. ILLINGWORTH KAY. Cr. 8vo. 5s. net. [Immediately.

JOHNSON (EFFIE).

IN THE FIRE, AND OTHER FANCIES. Frontispiece by WALTER CRANE. 500 copies, imp. 16mo. 3s. 6d. net.

JOHNSON (LIONEL).

THE ART OF THOMAS HARDY. Six Essays, with etched portrait by WM. STRANG, and bibliography by JOHN LANE, cr. 8vo. 5s. 6d. net.
Also 150 copies, large paper, with proofs of the portrait.
£1. 1s. net. [*Very Shortly.*

JOHNSON (LIONEL).

A VOLUME OF POEMS, fcap. 8vo. 5s. net. [*In preparation.*

KEATS (JOHN).

THREE ESSAYS, now issued in book form for the first time. Edited by H. BUXTON FORMAN, with life mask by HAYDON. Fcap. 4to. 10s. 6d. net. [*Very few remain.*

LEATHER (R. K.).

VERSES. 250 copies, fcap. 8vo. 3s. net.
Transferred by the Author to the present Publishers.

LEATHER (R. K.), & RICHARD LE GALLIENNE.

THE STUDENT AND THE BODY-SNATCHER, AND OTHER TRIFLES. [*Small paper edition out of print.*
There remain a very few of the 50 large paper copies.
7s. 6d. net.

LE GALLIENNE (RICHARD).

PROSE FANCIES, with a portrait of the Author. 5s. net.
Also a limited large paper edition. 12s. 6d. net.
[*In preparation.*

LE GALLIENNE (RICHARD).

THE BOOK BILLS OF NARCISSUS. An account rendered by RICHARD LE GALLIENNE. 2nd edition, cr. 8vo., buckram. 3s. 6d. net.

LE GALLIENNE (RICHARD).

ENGLISH POEMS. 3rd edition, cr. 8vo. 5s. net.

LE GALLIENNE (RICHARD).

GEORGE MEREDITH ; Some Characteristics ; with a Bibliography (much enlarged) by JOHN LANE, portrait, &c. 3rd edition, cr. 8vo.   5s. 6d. net.

LE GALLIENNE (RICHARD).

THE RELIGION OF A LITERARY MAN.   Cr. 8vo.   4th thousand.   3s. 6d. net.
Also a special rubricated edition on hand-made paper. 8vo.   10s. 6d. net.

LETTERS TO LIVING ARTISTS.

500 copies, fcap. 8vo.   3s. 6d. net.   [Very few remain.

MARSTON (PHILIP BOURKE).

A LAST HARVEST : LYRICS AND SONNETS FROM THE BOOK OF LOVE.   Edited by LOUISE CHANDLER MOULTON.   500 copies, fcap. 8vo.   5s. net.
Also 50 copies on large paper, hand-made.   10s. 6d. net.
[Very few remain.

MARTIN (W. WILSEY).

QUATRAINS, LIFE'S MYSTERY, AND OTHER POEMS. 16mo.   2s. 6d. net.   [Very few remain.

MARZIALS (THEO.).

THE GALLERY OF PIGEONS, AND OTHER POEMS.   Fcap. 8vo.   4s. 6d. net.   [Very few remain.
Transferred by the Author to the present Publishers.

MEYNELL (MRS.) (ALICE C. THOMPSON).

POEMS.   2nd edition, fcap. 8vo.   3s. 6d. net.   A few of the 50 large paper copies (1st edition) remain.   12s. 6d. net.

MEYNELL (MRS.).

THE RHYTHM OF LIFE, AND OTHER ESSAYS.   2nd Edition, fcap. 8vo.   3s. 6d. net.   A few of the 50 large paper copies (1st edition) remain.   12s. 6d. net.

MURRAY (ALMA).

PORTRAIT AS BEATRICE CENCI.   With critical notice, containing four letters from ROBERT BROWNING. 8vo. wrapper. 2s. *net.*

NETTLESHIP (J. T.).

ROBERT BROWNING. Essays and Thoughts. Third edition, cr. 8vo. 5s. 6d. *net. In preparation.* Half a dozen of the Whatman L.P. copies (first edition) remain. £1. 1s. *net.*

NOBLE (JAS. ASHCROFT).

THE SONNET IN ENGLAND, AND OTHER ESSAYS. Title-page and cover design by AUSTIN YOUNG. 600 copies. cr. 8vo. 5s. *net.*
Also 50 copies L.P. 12s. 6d. *net.*

NOEL (HON. RODEN).

POOR PEOPLE'S CHRISTMAS. 250 copies. 16mo. 1s. *net.*
[*Very few remain.*

OXFORD CHARACTERS.

A series of lithographed portraits by WILL ROTHENSTEIN, with text by F. YORK POWELL and others. To be issued monthly in term. Each part will contain two portraits. Part I. contains portraits of Sir Henry Acland and Mr. W. A. L. Fletcher, and Part II. of Mr. Robinson F. Ellis and Lord St. Cyres. Folio, 200 copies. 5s *net* per part. Also 25 special copies, containing proofs of the portraits, signed by the artist. 10s. 6d. *net* per part.

PINKERTON (PERCY).

GALEAZZO : a Venetian Episode, and other Poems. Etched frontispiece. 16mo. 5s. *net.*   [*Very few remain.*
Transferred by the Author to the present Publishers.

RADFORD (DOLLIE).

SONGS. A new volume of verse.   [*In preparation.*

RADFORD (ERNEST).

CHAMBERS TWAIN. Frontispiece by WALTER CRANE. 250 copies. Imp. 16mo. 5s. *net.*
Also 50 copies large paper. 10s. 6d. *net.* [*Very few remain.*

RHYMERS' CLUB, THE BOOK OF THE.

A second series is in preparation. 16mo. 5s. *net.*

SCHAFF (DR. P.).

LITERATURE AND POETRY: Papers on Dante, etc. Portrait and Plates. 100 copies only. 8vo. 10s. *net.*

SCOTT (WILLIAM BELL).

A POET'S HARVEST HOME: WITH AN AFTERMATH. 300 copies, fcap. 8vo. 5s. *net.* [*Out of print.*
*** *Will not be reprinted.*

SHAW (A. D. L.).

THE HAPPY WANDERER: Poems. Fcap. 8vo. 5s. *net.*
[*In preparation.*

STODDARD (R. H.).

THE LION'S CUB: WITH OTHER VERSE. Portrait. 100 copies only, bound in an illuminated Persian design. Fcap. 8vo. 5s. *net.* [*Very few remain.*

SYMONDS (JOHN ADDINGTON).

IN THE KEY OF BLUE, AND OTHER PROSE ESSAYS. Cover design by C. S. RICKETTS. 2nd edition, thick cr. 8vo. 8s. 6d. *net.*

THOMPSON (FRANCIS).

A VOLUME OF POEMS. With frontispiece, title page, and cover design by LAURENCE HOUSMAN. 2nd edition, pott 4to. 5s. *net.*

TODHUNTER (JOHN).

A SICILIAN IDYLL. Frontispiece by WALTER CRANE. 250 copies. Imp. 16mo 5s. *net.*
Also 50 copies on hand-made large paper, fcap. 4to. 10s. 6d. *net.* [*Very few remain.*

TOMSON (GRAHAM R.).

> AFTER SUNSET. A volume of Poems. With title page and
> cover design by R. ANNING BELL. Fcap. 8vo. 5s. net.
> Also a limited large paper edition. 12s. 6d. net.
> *[In preparation.*

TREE (H. BEERBOHM).

> THE IMAGINATIVE FACULTY. A Lecture delivered at the
> Royal Institution. With portrait of MR. TREE from
> an unpublished drawing by the MARCHIONESS OF
> GRANBY. Fcap. 8vo., boards. 2s. 6d. net.

TYNAN HINKSON (KATHARINE).

> CUCKOO SONGS. With title page and cover design by
> LAURENCE HOUSMAN. 500 copies, fcap. 8vo. 5s. net.
> *[In preparation.*

VAN DYKE (HENRY).

> THE POETRY OF TENNYSON. 3rd edition, enlarged, cr.
> 8vo. 5s. 6d. net.
>
> *The late Laureate himself gave valuable aid in correcting
> various details.*

WATSON (WILLIAM).

> THE ELOPING ANGELS : A CAPRICE. Second edition,
> sq. 16mo. buckram. 3s. 6d. net.

WATSON (WILLIAM).

> EXCURSIONS IN CRITICISM : BEING SOME PROSE RECREA-
> TIONS OF A RHYMER. 2nd edition, cr. 8vo. 5s. net.

WATSON (WILLIAM).

> THE PRINCE'S QUEST, AND OTHER POEMS. With a
> bibliographical note added. 2nd edition, fcap. 8vo.
> 4s. 6d. net.

WEDMORE (FREDERICK).

> PASTORALS OF FRANCE—RENUNCIATIONS. A volume of
> Stories. Title-page by JOHN FULLEYLOVE, R.I. 3rd
> edition, cr. 8vo. 5s. net.
>
> *A few of the large paper copies of Renunciations* (1st Edition)
> *remain.* 10s. 6d. net.

WICKSTEED (P. H.).

> DANTE : SIX SERMONS. 3rd edition, cr. 8vo. 2s. net.

WILDE (OSCAR).

THE SPHINX. A poem decorated throughout in line and colour, and bound in a design by CHARLES RICKETTS. 250 copies. £2. 2s. *net.* 25 copies large paper. £5. 5s. *net.* [*Shortly.*

WILDE (OSCAR).

The incomparable and ingenious history of Mr. W. H., being the true secret of Shakespear's sonnets now for the first time here fully set forth, with initial letters and cover design by CHARLES RICKETTS. 500 copies. 10s. 6d. *net.* Also 50 copies large paper. 21s. *net.*
[*In preparation.*

WILDE (OSCAR).

DRAMATIC WORKS, now printed for the first time with a specially designed binding to each volume by CHARLES SHANNON. 500 copies, sm. 4to. 7s. 6d. *net* per vol. Also 50 copies large paper. 15s. *net* per vol.
Vol. I. LADY WINDERMERE'S FAN. A comedy in four acts. [*Ready.*
Vol. II. A WOMAN OF NO IMPORTANCE. A comedy in four acts. [*Shortly.*
Vol. III. THE DUCHESS OF PADUA. A blank verse tragedy in five acts. [*Shortly.*

WILDE (OSCAR).

SALOME. A Tragedy in one Act, done into English, with title page, 10 illustrations, tail piece, and cover design by AUBREY BEARDSLEY. 500 copies, sm. 4to. 15s. *net.* Also 100 copies large paper. 30s. *net.* [*Shortly.*

WYNNE (FRANCES).

WHISPER. A volume of Verse. Fcap. 8vo. 2s. 6d. *net. Transferred by the Author to the present Publishers.*

A Memoir by KATHARINE TYNAN, and a portrait, have been added.

The Hobby Horse

A new series of this illustrated magazine will be published quarterly by subscription, under the Editorship of HERBERT P. HORNE. Subscription £1 per annum, post free, for the four numbers. Quarto, printed on hand-made paper, and issued in a limited edition to subscribers only. The Magazine will contain articles upon Literature, Music, Painting, Sculpture, Architecture, and the Decorative Arts; Poems; Essays; Fiction; original Designs; with reproductions of pictures and drawings by the old masters and contemporary artists. There will be a new title-page and ornaments designed by the Editor. Among the contributors to the Hobby Horse are:

The late MATTHEW ARNOLD.
LAURENCE BINYON.
WILFRID BLUNT.
FORD MADOX BROWN.
The late ARTHUR BURGESS.
E. BURNE-JONES, A.R.A.
AUSTIN DOBSON.
RICHARD GARNETT, LL.D.
A. J. HIPKINS, F.S.A.
SELWYN IMAGE.
LIONEL JOHNSON.
RICHARD LE GALLIENNE.
SIR F. LEIGHTON, Bart., P.R.A.
T. HOPE MCLACHLAN.
MAY MORRIS.
C. HUBERT H. PARRY, Mus. Doc.
A. W. POLLARD.

F. YORK POWELL.
CHRISTINA G. ROSSETTI.
W. M. ROSSETTI.
JOHN RUSKIN, D.C.L., LL.D.
FREDERICK SANDYS.
The late W. BELL SCOTT.
FREDERICK J. SHIELDS.
J H. SHORTHOUSE.
The late JAMES SMETHAM.
SIMEON SOLOMON.
A. SOMERVELL.
The late J. ADDINGTON SYMONDS.
KATHARINE TYNAN.
G. F. WATTS, R.A.
FREDERICK WEDMORE.
OSCAR WILDE.

Prospectuses on Application.

THE BODLEY HEAD, VIGO STREET, LONDON, W.

'Nearly every book put out by Messrs. Elkin Mathews and John Lane, at the Sign of the Bodley Head, is a satisfaction to the special senses of the modern bookman, for bindings, shapes, types, and papers. They have surpassed themselves, and registered a real achievement in English bookmaking by the volume of " Poems, Dramatic and Lyrical," of Lord De Tabley.'
Newcastle Daily Chronicle.

'A ray of hopefulness is stealing again into English poetry after the twilight greys of Clough, Arnold, and Tennyson. Even unbelief wears braver colours. Despite the jeremiads, which are the dirges of the elder gods, England is still a nest of singing-birds (*teste* the Catalogue of Elkin Mathews and John Lane).'—Mr. ZANGWILL, in *Pall Mall Magazine.*

' One can nearly always be certain, when one sees on the title-page of any given book the name of Messrs. Elkin Mathews and John Lane as being the publishers thereof, that there will be something worth reading to be found between the boards.'— *World.*

' All Messrs. Mathews and Lane's books are so beautifully printed and so tastefully issued, that it rejoices the heart of a book-lover to handle them ; but they have shewn their sound judgment not less markedly in the literary quality of their publications. The choiceness of form is not inappropriate to the matter, which is always of something more than ephemeral worth. This was a distinction on which the better publishers at one time prided themselves ; they never lent their names to trash ; but some names associated with worthy traditions have proved more than once a delusion and a snare. The record of Messrs. Elkin Mathews and John Lane is perfect in this respect, and their imprint is a guarantee of the worth of what they publish.'—*Birmingham Daily Post, Nov. 6th*, 1893.

www.ingramcontent.com/pod-product-compliance
Lightning Source LLC
Chambersburg PA
CBHW030628270326
41927CB00007B/1353